Welcome to Planet Earth

Written by *Simon Blanchard*
illustrated by *Rebecca Flitcroft*

**Grosvenor House
Publishing Limited**

The right of Simon Blanchard to be identified as the author of this
work has been asserted in accordance with Section 78
of the Copyright, Designs and Patents Act 1988

The book cover is copyright to Simon Blanchard

This book is published by
Grosvenor House Publishing Ltd
Link House
140 The Broadway, Tolworth, Surrey, KT6 7HT.
www.grosvenorhousepublishing.co.uk

A CIP record for this book
is available from the British Library

This book is a work of fiction. Any resemblance to
people or events, past or present, is purely coincidental.

ISBN: 978-1-83975-539-2

*"The world is not respectable.
It is mortal, tormented, confused, deluded
forever, but it is shot through with beauty,
with love, with glints of courage and
laughter."*

George Santayana (1863-1952).

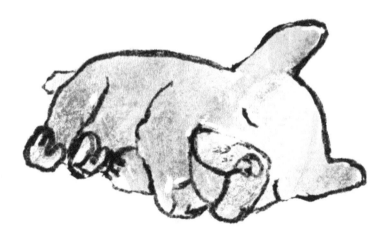

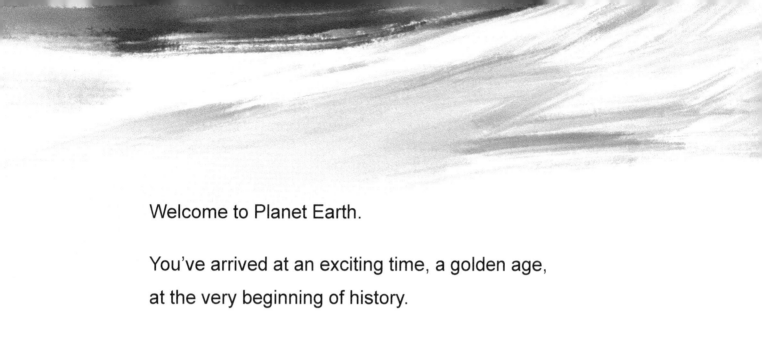

Welcome to Planet Earth.

You've arrived at an exciting time, a golden age,
at the very beginning of history.

"All the past is just the beginning of a beginning;
all that the human mind has accomplished is but
the dream before the awakening." (H G Wells.)

Our wish is that you have the wisdom, courage and generosity to add to the common good. This seems to be the essence of a life well lived and we believe your own flourishing will follow naturally.

We are made of stardust…

...the elements that all living things are made of are forged when giant stars explode.

These supernovas, which shine briefly with the brightness of a billion suns, occur perhaps once every hundred years per galaxy. And yet, because of the vastness of the universe, there are about 30 per second... 'the universe is bubbling like champagne.' (Caspar Henderson)

Your arrival itself is a miracle, our family tree goes back millions of years. Once we had gills, once a forked tongue, once we were furry, once we lived underground.

And yet, remarkably, none of our ancestors got trampled, were mortally wounded, frozen or struck by a meteor before they passed on that tiny genetic code that has led to you!

Hopefully you'll get a chance to learn history. It's brimming with amazing stories... look out for Nelson Mandela, Martin Luther King, Mahatma Gandhi...

...Emmeline Pankhurst, Isaac Newton, Rosa Parks and so many others.

History is at its most powerful when it shows us the big picture. Its gift is to help us to see the world more clearly.

We are learning to care for the planet; protecting the oceans, forests and wild places; learning to deflect meteors, avoid catastrophes and explore a universe so vast that it boggles even the brightest minds.

"The world is full of magical things patiently waiting for our wits to grow sharper." Bertrand Russell.

Perhaps you'll study science and learn the amazing fact that it all started with an almighty bang about 13.8 billion years ago.

From a tiny dot our universe was born. And now on a rapidly spinning planet, circling an average star, in one of billions of galaxies some frail creatures have evolved the brain power to explore its vastness and begin to understand its laws.
It is as though the giant universe is gradually opening an eye, perhaps for the first time.

Look carefully and you'll see that people are beginning to care about humans on the other side of the planet. In fact, we are caring for the whole planet. Our circle of empathy is widening - to not just extend to our families, communities, nations; but to go beyond and encompass the whole world.

"The world is my country; all mankind are my brethren and to do good is my religion." Thomas Paine (1737-1809).

Imagine all the people you might meet. Imagine all the friends you could have. All shapes and sizes, nationalities, religions, rich and poor, old and young. People to learn from and care for, to share laughter and sadness with...

You may get the chance to travel.

Maybe you'll want to walk the glass walkway thousands of feet up on the side of Tianmen Mountain, fly across New Zealand's glaciers, sit quietly in a Buddhist temple or cross the skybridge in Norway.

Perhaps to see the snow-capped mountains of the Karakoram, the dancing birds of paradise in the depths of the tropical jungle, dolphins in the azure blue waters of the Indian Ocean or herds of elephants migrating across the Serengeti.

You'll be able to learn how chemistry becomes biology and then life evolves. There isn't a corner of the planet where life hasn't evolved in wondrous diversity...

...from tardigrades, little water bears, that can survive in the hottest and coldest environments on earth; to tiny hummingbirds that live in the sun-drenched tropics and require a constant supply of nectar; to the rarely seen giant squid at home thousands of feet below the ocean's surface.

Our planet boasts 5,400 mammal species alone; from blue whales weighing as much as a herd of elephants to the bumblebee bat weighing less than a one pence piece.

You've arrived at a time when we are learning to live in harmony with nature. Big heroes and little heroes have fought to raise life expectancy and reduce poverty...

...now our heroes are fighting to finish the job and make sure it's sustainable. In more developed countries rivers are cleaner, the air is less polluted and wildlife is returning.

Any future is possible. It's up to us.

Look out for music, poetry, art; they can make the mundane magical, connect across ages and cultures, bring happiness, turn depression into sorrow, let you feel what it is to be human, deepen your understanding...

You'll be able to study literature. Stories from different times and places written by the greatest minds, laying bare the intricacies and complexities of the human condition.

Exploring, revealing and entertaining; sometimes tragic, sometimes comic, sometimes scary, sometimes romantic, sometimes epic...

Every human born is a treasure: a potential problem solver, creator, friend, carer, ocean-cleaner, someone who can add to the stock of common good many times and in many ways.

"How far that little candle throws his beams! So shines a good deed in a weary world."
William Shakespeare (1564-1616).

Lightning Source UK Ltd.
Milton Keynes UK
UKHW051944041021
391649UK00002B/68